# TAUNTON
# TO
# BARNSTAPLE

**Vic Mitchell and Keith Smith**

**MP** Middleton Press

*Cover picture: The shunter is about to uncouple class 4300 no. 7319 from its train at Barnstaple Junction after arrival from Taunton on 24th June 1960. (N.L.Browne)*

Published September 1995
Reprinted June 2001
Second reprint October 2004

ISBN  1 873793 60 X

© Middleton Press, 1995

Design       Deborah Esher
Typesetting  Barbara Mitchell

Published by
            Middleton Press
            Easebourne Lane
            Midhurst, West Sussex
            GU29 9AZ
Tel: 01730 813169
Fax: 01730 812601
Email: info@middletonpress.co.uk
www.middletonpress.co.uk

Printed & bound by Biddles Ltd, Kings Lynn

# CONTENTS

# ACKNOWLEDGEMENTS

We would like to express our thanks for help so willingly given by many of the photographers mentioned in the captions and also W.R.Burton, G.Croughton, P.Gower, N.Langridge, M.King, C.Maggs, National Railway Museum Library, G.T.Reardon, E.Youldon, Mr.D. & Dr.S.Salter and our ever helpful wives.

**Barnstaple station names**
A "Junction" 1874 to 1971
B "Victoria Road" from 1949
C "Town" from 1886
Dashes indicate freight only.

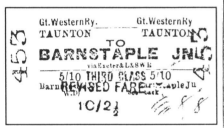

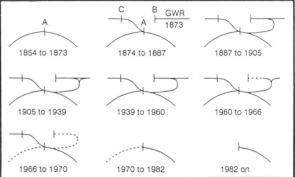

1854 to 1873    1874 to 1887    1887 to 1905
1905 to 1939    1939 to 1960    1960 to 1966
1966 to 1970    1970 to 1982    1982 on

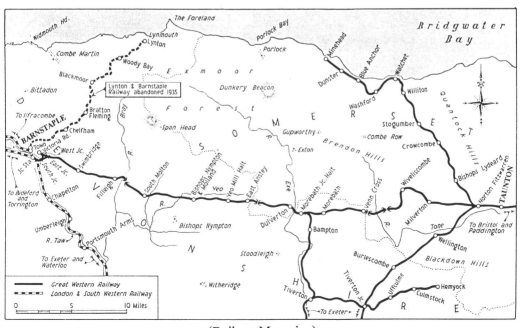

(Railway Magazine)

# GEOGRAPHICAL SETTING

From Taunton to Norton Fitzwarren the route is close to the east-flowing River Tone. The line continues through the Vale of Taunton Deane to Wiveliscombe, following a tributary of the Tone west of Milverton. This climb is followed by a descent into the valley of the upper reaches of the Tone which is crossed on a viaduct before reaching Venn Cross.

An undulating course across the various headwaters of the River Batherm takes the line into the Exe Valley, the river being crossed shortly before reaching Dulverton station (two miles south of Dulverton). There follows a climb up the narrow valley of the Brockey River, over a watershed and into the Yeo Valley. A descent close to this river continues to within two miles of South Molton, the app-

roach necessitating a climb over a ridge into the valley of the River Mole.

There follows a further rise and fall to cross the deep valley of the River Bray and yet another climb before starting the steep descent to the Taw Valley at Barnstaple.

The geology is particularly varied as far as Wiveliscombe, various red sandstones and marls predominating. Most of the remainder of the route is on the Devonian Sandstones of the foothills of Exmoor.

The crossing of the boundaries between Somerset and Devon are mentioned in the captions.

The location maps are to the scale of 1" to 1 mile and are from the 1930 edition. The other maps are at 25" to 1 mile, unless otherwise indicated.

# HISTORICAL BACKGROUND

The broad gauge Bristol & Exeter Railway was opened in stages westwards reaching Taunton on 1st July 1842 and Exeter on 1st May 1844.

The first railway at Barnstaple was a horse worked line for mineral traffic from docks downstream from the town at Fremington. It opened on 25th April 1848. The first passenger trains ran on 1st August 1855 and were on a broad gauge line from Crediton to Freming-

ton. This service was extended to Bideford in 1855. The Minehead branch was opened to Watchet in 1862 and completed in 1874.

The Devon & Somerset Railway's Act was passed on 29th July 1864 and the first section from a junction near the village of Norton Fitzwarren to Wiveliscombe was opened on 8th June 1871. It was a single line of broad gauge track and was operated by the BER. The remainder of the route to the terminus at

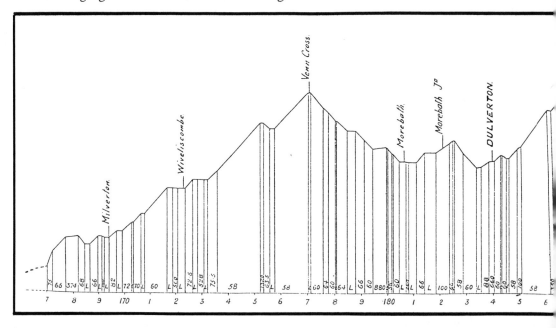

Barnstaple came into use on 1st November 1873.

The Great Western Railway acquired both the BER and the DSR in 1876. Conversion of the Norton Fitzwarren-Barnstaple line to standard gauge took place in May 1881.

The single line from Tiverton to Morebath Junction opened on 1st August 1884 and the connection between the GWR and the London & South Western Railway at Barnstaple followed on 1st June 1887. The changes in the Barnstaple area are summarised in the diagram above the route map.

The route became part of the Western Region of British Railways in January 1948. Barnstaple (Victoria Road) was closed to passengers on 13th June 1960, when trains were diverted to Barnstaple Junction.

Taunton-Barnstaple services were withdrawn entirely on 3rd October 1966.

# PASSENGER SERVICES

Down trains running at least five days per week are considered in this section.

The initial service to Wiveliscombe was six trains, calling at all stations, weekdays only. Extension to Barnstaple brought the same frequency but one train omitted many stops.

The August 1893 timetable showed five stopping trains, one non-stop and one stopping only at Dulverton, weekdays only. A similar pattern was worked in 1913, the 4.15 pm arrival at Barnstaple carrying a "Luncheon Car" from Paddington (depart 11.50am). Twenty years later, there were still five slow trains but there was an extra semi-fast service.

Sunday working was uncommon; such services did appear in the summers of 1878 and 1936 to 1939.

The summers of 1923 and 1924 had nine trains, four of which had limited stops. By 1939 this had been reduced to seven but there was one to Wiveliscombe and another as far as Dulverton.

The wartime timetables mostly had five stopping trains only, with a morning trip for much of the 1940s to Venn Cross, returning at 8.0am. During the 1950s, the basic service rose to seven stopping trains, with a 5.45pm from Taunton to Dulverton added for many years on Mondays to Fridays. On summer Saturdays there were five or six extra trains. Several ran through to Ilfracombe, originating at Manchester, Wolverhampton, Cardiff or London.

The basic service in the 1960s comprised six trains, two of which ran through to Torrington following the introduction of DMUs in September 1964. By the summer of 1965, there were only three additional trains on Saturdays, these missing out the smaller stations. The same frequency applied in the final summer, but there were no longer any through trains.

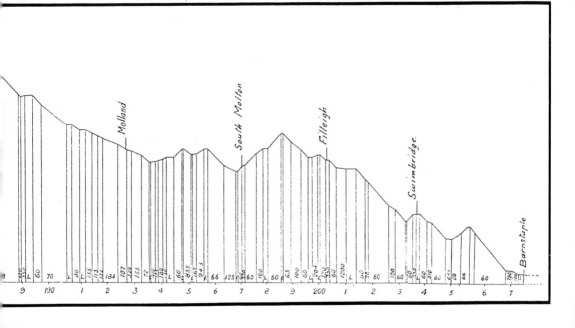

# TAUNTON

1. The first station consisted of two platforms, end to end, on the south side of the line, both having roofs extending over the track. This arrangement was altered when through running commenced and in 1868 the station was rebuilt with three through tracks with a roof over them. Alterations in 1931 involved retaining the original down platform (right), providing an island platform and building a new up through platform, together with some bays. (Lens of Sutton)

The 1930 map includes the overall roof (right) and the avoiding line (lower right) which was used mainly by goods trains. At peak holiday times, some through passenger trains stopped on it to change locomotives. The cattle pens of West Yard are marked.

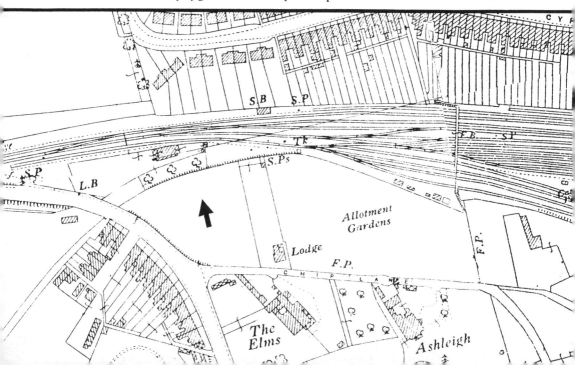

2.    Chard trains usually used platform 2;
Minehead and Barnstaple arrivals were at
platform 8, with departures from 3 or 4, which
were also used by some stopping trains for
Exeter. Local trains for Yeovil and Bristol
mainly used the up bay, no. 9. (S.P.Derek)

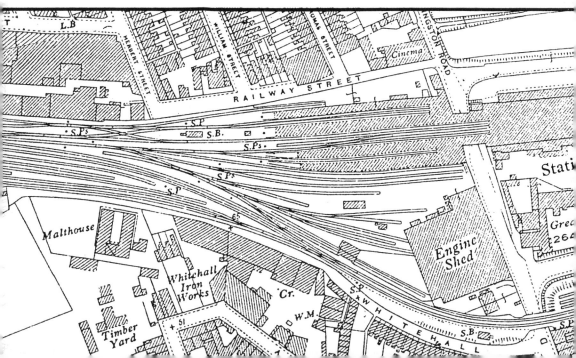

3. The island platform received most long distance trains although such facilities as the refreshment rooms and bookstalls were on platforms 1 and 7. On Saturdays in the summer of 1957, 170 expresses called or passed through the station, less than half being to or from London. (Lens of Sutton)

4. An April 1963 photograph includes the engine shed (right) and class 4300 2-6-0 no. 6372 at the double faced platform 3, with a Barnstaple train. The DMU is waiting to depart for Minehead from platform 4. (C.L.Caddy coll.)

5. Barnstaple Junction is the destination of no. 7320, a later member of the 4300 class. It is blowing off ready to leave at 5.45pm on 15th August 1964. The pleasant evening amble would end at 7.30. (E.Wilmshurst)

July 1924

## LONDON, TAUNTON, DULVERTON, BARNSTAPLE, and ILFRACOMBE.—Great Western.

### Down. — Week Days only.

| Miles | Down. | ngt | mrn | mrn | aft | aft | aft | aft | aft | aft | aft | aft |
|---|---|---|---|---|---|---|---|---|---|---|---|---|
| 12 | London (Pad.)....dep. | 12B0 | 5 30 | 9 0 | .... | 12 5 | 1 30 | .... | 3 30 | .... | 4 30 | 6 30 | |
| — | Taunton.....dep. | 8 0 | 1015 | 1212 | 1 10 | 3 7 | 4 35 | 5 35 | 6 5 | .... | 8 0 | 1115 |
| 2 | Norton Fitzwarren....dep. | 8 5 | 1020 | .... | 1 15 | .... | 5 48 | .... | 8 6 | 1120 | | |
| 6½ | Milverton | 8 15 | 1030 | .... | 1 26 | .... | 5 58 | .... | 8 16 | 1130 | | |
| 9½ | Wiveliscombe | 8 24 | 1038 | .... | 1 34 | 3 24 | 5 56 | 7 | .... | 8 24 | 1137 | |
| 14½ | Venn Cross | 8 35 | 1049 | .... | 1 45 | .... | 6 18 | .... | 8 35 | | | |
| 17½ | Morebath | 8 44 | 1056 | .... | 1 54 | .... | 6 25 | .... | 8 43 | | | |
| 21 | Dulverton 57 | 8 54 | 11 6 | 1 0 | 2 5 | 4 2 | 5 24 | 6 23 | 6 53 | 7 15 | 8 53 | |
| 24½ | East Anstey ....[Molland | 9 4 | 1118 | .... | 2 15 | .... | 5 33 | .... | 7 25 | 9 4 | | |
| 30 | Bishop's Nympton and | 9 14 | 1127 | .... | 2 24 | .... | .... | 7 34 | 9 13 | | | |
| 34½ | South Molton | 9 24 | 1137 | .... | 2 34 | 4 30 | 5 54 | .... | 7 43 | 9 23 | | |
| 37½ | Filleigh | 9 33 | 1146 | .... | 2 44 | .... | .... | 7 52 | 9 32 | | | |
| 41 | Swimbridge | 9 42 | 1155 | .... | 2 54 | .... | .... | 8 0 | 9 41 | | | |
| 44½ | Barnstaple (G.W.) * 166 {arr. {dep. | 9 48 10 0 | 1211 1220 | .... | 3 10 .... | .... | 553 10 4 | 59 6 22 | .... | 7 44 | 8 6 9 47 | 9 30 |
| 45½ | Barnstaple J. 166....arr. | 10 5 | 1225 | 1 55 | 3 84 | 576 21 | .... | 7 54 | .... | | | |
| 60½ | Ilfracombe 166.... " | 1116 | 2 10 | 2 45 | 4 2 | 85 57 | 7 15 | .... | 8 32 | 9A43 | | |

*Saturdays only.*

### Up. — Week Days only.

| Mls | Up. | mrn | mrn | S | mrn | mrn | aft | mrn | aft | aft | aft | aft |
|---|---|---|---|---|---|---|---|---|---|---|---|---|
| — | Ilfracombe....dep. | .... | .... | 8 50 | 9 15 | .... | 1140 | 1 35 | 2 55 | 4 25 | 8 0 | |
| 15 | Barnstaple Jun. .... " | .... | .... | 9 35 | 10 15 | .... | 1235 | 2 44 | 3 55 | 5 40 | 8 30 | |
| 16 | Barnstaple {arr. (G.W.) * ....{dep. | 7 0 | 8 34 | .... | 10 20 | 1050 | 1235 | 3 0 | .... | 6 0 | 8 55 | |
| 19½ | Swimbridge | 7 9 | 8 43 | .... | .... | 1059 | .... | 3 9 | .... | 6 10 | 9 4 | |
| 23½ | Filleigh | 7 18 | 8 52 | .... | .... | 11 8 | .... | 3 19 | .... | 6 22 | 9 13 | |
| 26½ | South Molton...[Molland | 7 28 | 9 2 | .... | 10 56 | 1118 | .... | 3 31 | 4 32 | 6 35 | 9 22 | |
| 30½ | Bishop's Nympton and | 7 36 | 9 13 | .... | .... | 1128 | .... | 3 41 | .... | 6 45 | 9 30 | |
| 36 | East Anstey | 7 47 | 9 24 | .... | 11 17 | 1139 | .... | 3 53 | .... | 7 3 | 9 41 | |
| 39½ | Dulverton 57 | 7 56 | 9 33 | 1040 | 11 31 | 1146 | 12 51 | 4 0 | 4 65 | 5 7 | 1 8 | 9 49 |
| 43 | Morebath | 8 5 | 9 43 | .... | .... | 1214 | .... | 4 16 | .... | 7 2 | 8 9 | 58 |
| 46½ | Venn Cross | 8 13 | 9 51 | .... | .... | 1223 | .... | 4 26 | .... | 7 37 | 10 6 | |
| 51½ | Wiveliscombe | 8 25 | 10 2 | .... | 11 50 | 1235 | .... | 4 37 | .... | 7 48 | 1015 | |
| 54½ | Milverton | 8 32 | 1010 | .... | 12 10 | 1243 | .... | 4 43 | .... | 7 56 | 1022 | |
| 58½ | Norton Fitzwarren....22 | 8 42 | 1020 | .... | .... | 1252 | .... | 4 57 | .... | 8 6 | .... | |
| 60½ | Taunton 7, 17, 22 ....arr. | 8 47 | 1025 | 1133 | 12 22 | 1257 | 2 30 | 5 2 5 | 46 | 8 11 | 1033 | |
| 203¼ | 17 London (Pad.)....arr. | .... | 1 18 | .... | 4 5 | .... | 5 30 | 9 0 | 9 0 | 1115 | 7 10 | |

*Through Train to Bristol.*

A Passengers find their own way between Barnstaple Junction and Barnstaple Station.

B Leaves Paddington at 10 aft. on Sundays.

K Slip Carriage.

P Arrives at 4 aft. on Saturdays.

S Saturdays only.

* Over ¼ mile to Barnstaple Town Station.

6. There were five signal boxes in the station area, these closing progressively from July 1963 to March 1987. West Station Box is visible as the 10.40 Leeds to Paignton leaves behind no. 45045 on 26th February 1977. (T.Heavyside)

7. A westward view in 1990 from former bays 3 and 4 includes the footbridge shown on the map but little else from the past. There were still four through lines but the island platform was out of use. (V.Mitchell)

8. Seen from the footbridge on 26th April 1983 is no. 45063 with an up parcels train. On the left are the connections to West Yard and beyond the bridge another group of sidings fan out to form Fairwater Permanent Way Depot. Quadruple track from Cogload Junction (four miles east of the station) to Norton Fitzwarren came into use in 1931-32. (T.Heavyside)

9. The west end of Fairwater sidings are in the foreground as no. 45040 passes with the 14.20 Paignton to Nottingham on 23rd July 1983. The rear coach partially obscures Silk Mill Crossing Box, beyond which were extensive sidings for a Government store established in 1940 and soon taken over by the US Army. It was known as G50, later as Blinkhorn Yard, and was on the up side. (D.Mitchell)

# NORTON FITZWARREN

10. Although there had been a junction here since 1862, the station did not come into use until 1st August 1873. The signal box is at the end of the down platform. The second box shown on the map was closed at an early date. (Lens of Sutton)

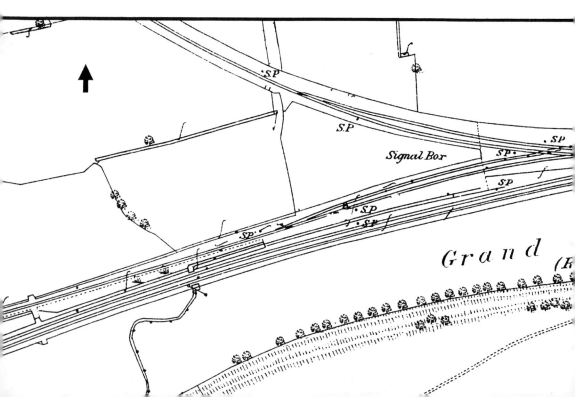

11. The main entrance was through the up side building and was close to the village centre. The roof of the Railway Hotel is on the right. The provision of a roof to the footbridge is unexpected, in view of the small number of people that would change trains here. (Lens of Sutton)

The first edition map includes an up goods loop and two sidings. The single line to Minehead is at the top and that to Barnstaple on the left. The Taunton-Exeter main line is from right to left.

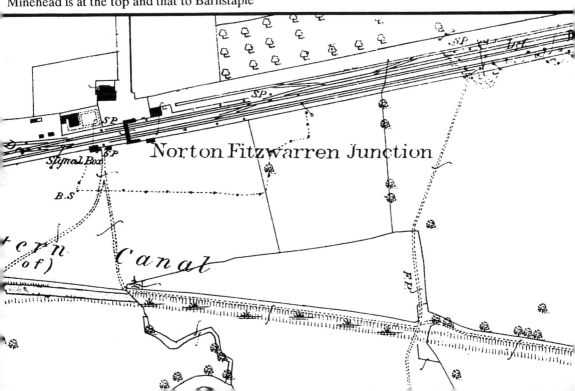

12. With the provision of quadruple track in 1931, four new platforms were built east of the original pair. A new 131-lever signal box (left) was opened on 14th February 1932, this remaining in use until 1st March 1970, when all points were taken out of use. An important development in 1937 was that the Barnstaple line's junction was revised so that it connected direct with the main line instead of into the Minehead branch. The goods yard and its 30cwt crane were in use until 6th July 1964. (Mowat coll.)

13. The rear two coaches of an up train are crossing the Minehead branch, our route to Barnstaple diverging behind them. The station closed on 30th October 1961, two years before this photograph was taken. (S.P.Derek)

14. As no. 47522 *Doncaster Enterprise* runs east with the Plymouth-Leeds vans on 2nd September 1989, we can see the then seldom used line to Minehead (right of locomotive) and the overgrown Barnstaple trackbed (left of last van). Subsequently, the single line has been used by some excursions to the West Somerset Railway, the first being from Manchester on 16th June 1990. (J.A.M.Vaughan)

15. Part of the Minehead single track was fenced off to form a private siding for the Taunton Cider Company, coming into use on 1st March 1983. It was occasionally used for WSR stock transfer. On 12th June 1991, no. 50002 was to be seen returning nos. D1035 and D7017 to Paignton from the WSR Gala. All cider traffic was forced onto the roads in December 1992. (D.Mitchell)

# MILVERTON

Ford Bridge
Quarry

Old Limekilns

S.P

S.P

Coal
Yard

Station

F.B.

S.P

S.B.

208

Ford Bridge

G.P

Mail A

Sluice

Lane

The 1930 map contains almost no features that are recognisable today. A roundabout was built near the site of the bridge and the A461 diverted along the trackbed, west of the station, to form a bypass for Milverton. It is now numbered B3227.

16. The historic St. Michael's Church on its hilltop location in the centre of the village is on the skyline in this charming postcard view. The population had been about 1500 during the first half of this century. (Lens of Sutton)

MILVERTON

17.  A passing loop was added here in about 1880. The van on the right is on a refuge siding. This and the loop were both extended in 1925 and again in 1936. (Lens of Sutton)

19.  This and the next picture were taken on 8th July 1959 and both feature 0-6-0PT no. 3736. The signal box dates from about 1903. A siding to serve the limeworks of William Thomas & Company was situated on the north side of the line between 1872 and 1884. (R.M.Casserley)

18.  The 2.44pm from Taunton is approaching on 8th July 1959, hauled by 2-6-0 no. 6375. The track from Norton Fitzwarren was doubled on 7th February 1937. (H.C.Casserley )

20. Included in this eastward view from the road bridge is the trailing crossover, a railwayman's vegetable allotment and two posts for automatic tablet transfer apparatus. (H.C.Casserley)

21. The ornate barge boards of the up waiting shelter are evident; less obvious is the bracket for the down main to sidings starting signal. The down intermediate starter is beyond the wagons, a third down signal being provided beyond that. (Lens of Sutton)

| Milverton | 1903 | 1933 |
|---|---|---|
| Passenger tickets issued | 14661 | 7464 |
| Season Tickets issued | - | 86 |
| Parcels forwarded | 4124 | 3249 |
| General goods forwarded (tons) | 1077 | 1121 |
| Coal and coke received | 366 | 120 |
| Other minerals received | 1619 | 99 |
| General goods received | 1620 | 645 |
| Trucks of livestock handled | 140 | 53 |

22. The crane appears to be mounted on a wagon. Most of the goods sheds on the route contained one of 30cwt capacity. The platform edge markings were unusual. (Lens of Sutton)

23. Featured here is the speed limit sign for down trains and the mechanism to prevent points being moved under a passing train. The bridge carried the A461. (E.Wilmshurst)

BRITISH RLYS (W)    BRITISH RLYS (W)
HALF DAY EXCURSION RETURN
Dulverton              Dulverton
TO
**TAUNTON**
AND BACK
THIRD CLASS
TAUNTON              TAUNTON
FOR CONDITIONS SEE BACK  E.B
0418    0418

25. The gate to the up platform was from a small approach road. The main approach was behind the signal box. Class 4300 2-6-0 no. 7337 is working the 8.12 am from Barnstaple Junction on 16th June 1963. (S.P.Derek)

24. The bracket signal had been removed by the time that no. 6372 was recorded with an up train on 15th June 1963. Note that telephone and telegram services were on offer. (E.Wilmshurst)

26. The goods yard closed on 30th September 1963 and much of the track was removed the following year. This June 1966 photograph shows the short lived facility for the permanent way trolley. Also included is the disused cattle dock. (C.L.Caddy)

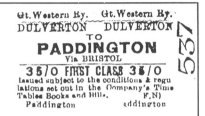

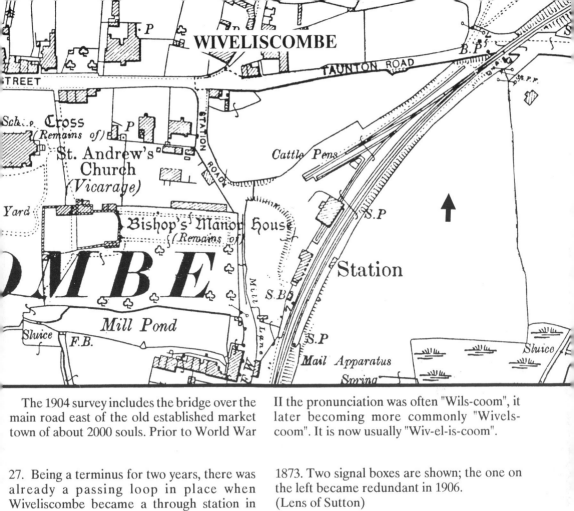

WIVELISCOMBE

The 1904 survey includes the bridge over the main road east of the old established market town of about 2000 souls. Prior to World War II the pronunciation was often "Wils-coom", it later becoming more commonly "Wivels-coom". It is now usually "Wiv-el-is-coom".

27. Being a terminus for two years, there was already a passing loop in place when Wiveliscombe became a through station in 1873. Two signal boxes are shown; the one on the left became redundant in 1906.
(Lens of Sutton)

28. The substantial water tank in the background was close to Town Mill and therefore a source of water. The large gap between the tracks was a legacy from the broad gauge era. (Lens of Sutton)

30. The 10.22am Swimbridge to Dulverton and Taunton freight passes through on 17th July 1963, hauled by class 3 2-6-2T no. 82008. Freight services at this station were withdrawn on 6th July 1964. (S.P.Derek)

29. The west elevation was photographed when the Taunton fare was 2/9$^d$. In 1995, the building was in commercial use, little changed. The March 1938 timetable showed an autotrain arriving here at 1.55pm on Thursdays and Saturdays and returning to Taunton at 2.5, a rare example of push-pull working on most of the route. (Lens of Sutton)

| Wiveliscombe | 1903 | 1933 |
| --- | --- | --- |
| Passenger tickets issued | 20613 | 11886 |
| Season Tickets issued | - | 130 |
| Parcels forwarded | 12000 | 11802 |
| General goods forwarded (tons) | 2035 | 1078 |
| Coal and coke received | 854 | 940 |
| Other minerals received | 3658 | 1707 |
| General goods received | 4435 | 5298 |
| Trucks of livestock handled | 302 | 398 |

31. Both locomotive water columns are included in this June 1963 picture. The nearer one has a brazier to reduce the risk of freezing. The facilities for gentlemen (left) froze regularly, as there was no roof. (E.Wilmshurst)

32. Class 4300 2-6-0 no. 7303 shows two lamps on the buffer beam to indicate an express working, probably to Ilfracombe. This route from London to that resort was quicker than the Southern Region route via Salisbury. (C.L.Caddy coll.)

33. No. 6345 works a local up train on a gloomy day in July 1964. The passing loop had been extended westward three times - in 1906, 1911 and 1939. The goods shed was still standing in 1995. (C.L.Caddy coll.)

34. A Barnstaple - bound train is about to enter the 445yd long Bathealton Tunnel on 25th September 1956. Having been built for broad gauge trains, clearances were more generous than normal. (H.C.Casserley)

# VENN CROSS

35.   The loop, up platform (left) and 31-lever signal box all date from 1905 when attempts were made to improve timekeeping on the long single line. The loop was extended westwards in 1937. Venn Cross Tunnel was 246 yds in length and is in the background of this 1963 photograph. (E.Wilmshurst)

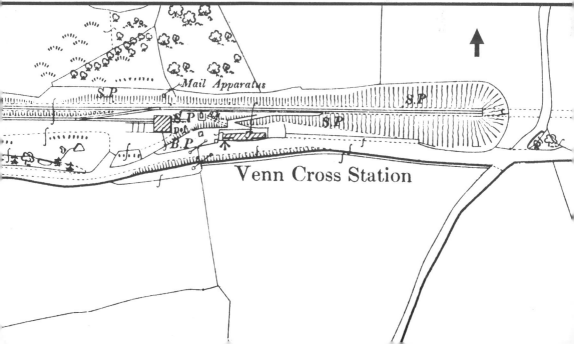

Venn Cross Station

36.  The footpath from the high level station building is visible, as is the curve in the up platform coping slabs to clear the buffer beams of locomotives using the points to the goods yard. The signalman is waiting to receive the tablet from the driver of no. 7333, which is arriving with the 1.15pm from Taunton on 17th July 1963. (S.P.Derek)

37.  At the east end of the station there were catch points (right) worked from the signal box and automatic spring points (foreground) on the down side. They were both to prevent run-aways entering the tunnel. Between the signal box and the shed, we pass into Devon. After closure, the building became a residence. At 666ft above sea level, the station was the second highest point on the route. (Lens of Sutton)

| Venn Cross | 1903 | 1933 |
|---|---|---|
| Passenger tickets issued | 3107 | 1405 |
| Season Tickets issued | - | 10 |
| Parcels forwarded | 2626 | 1004 |
| General goods forwarded (tons) | 340 | 143 |
| Coal and coke received | 17 | 74 |
| Other minerals received | 843 | 877 |
| General goods received | 1431 | 1125 |
| Trucks of livestock handled | 50 | 43 |

38.  Goods services were withdrawn on 30th September 1963 and the sidings lifted in 1964. No. 7337 was recorded soon after, waiting in the loop with a down "express". The small number of dwellings nearby would have generated few passengers. (C.L.Caddy coll.)

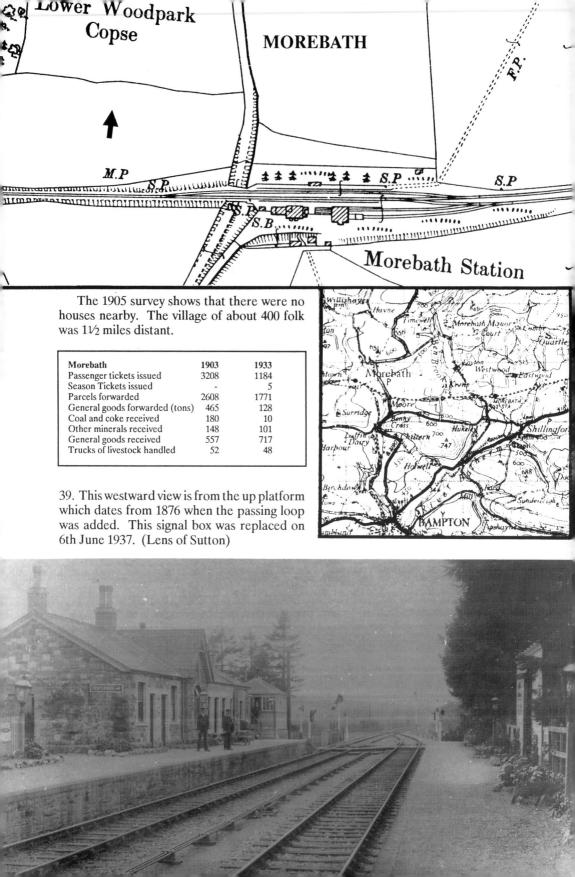

Lower Woodpark Copse

MOREBATH

M.P   S.P   S.P   S.P

S.P   S.B

Morebath Station

The 1905 survey shows that there were no houses nearby. The village of about 400 folk was 1½ miles distant.

| Morebath | 1903 | 1933 |
|---|---|---|
| Passenger tickets issued | 3208 | 1184 |
| Season Tickets issued | - | 5 |
| Parcels forwarded | 2608 | 1771 |
| General goods forwarded (tons) | 465 | 128 |
| Coal and coke received | 180 | 10 |
| Other minerals received | 148 | 101 |
| General goods received | 557 | 717 |
| Trucks of livestock handled | 52 | 48 |

39. This westward view is from the up platform which dates from 1876 when the passing loop was added. This signal box was replaced on 6th June 1937. (Lens of Sutton)

40. Still looking west we see the replacement signal box, which closed on 2nd March 1963, and the goods shed, which was taken out of use at the same time. The station was converted into a dwelling after closure. (Lens of Sutton)

41. The west end of the platforms had been extended in timber when the loop was lengthened in June 1937. Lightweight construction was necessary as they passed over a road onto an embankment. This is the scene in 1966, three years after the loop had been dispensed with. (C.L.Caddy)

# MOREBATH JUNCTION

42. The view from the eastbound train in September 1956 shows that the Exe Valley line branched from a loop on the main line. This loop had been extended at both ends in 1937. (H.C.Casserley)

43. Tablet exchange equipment is evident on 30th July 1963 as no. 6372 passes with the 5.55pm from Taunton. The branch to Exeter (right) closed completely on 7th October 1963 and the box and loop followed on 29th April 1964. (S.P.Derek)

# MOREBATH JUNCTION HALT

44. The halt was opened on 1st December 1928, west of the junction. The box and loop points are visible but the weary woman with a walking stick seems uninterested. (Lens of Sutton)

45. The halt was only a few minutes walk from the village and was built of durable concrete blocks. Hurricane lamps gave a slight glow at night. One mile to the west, we cross back into Somerset at Exebridge. (Lens of Sutton)

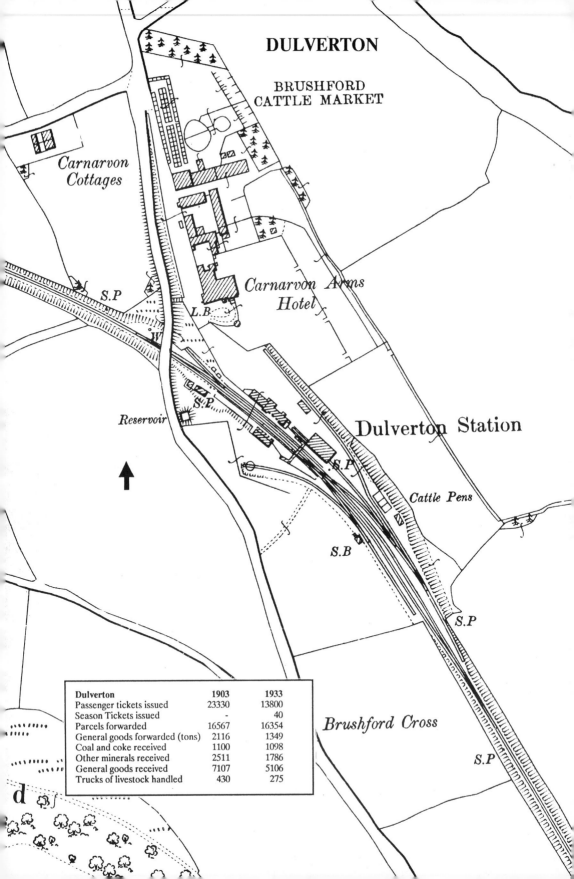

# DULVERTON

### BRUSHFORD
### CATTLE MARKET

*Carnarvon
Cottages*

S.P

*Carnarvon Arms
Hotel*

L.B.

*Reservoir*

S.P

Dulverton Station

*Cattle Pens*

S.B

S.P

*Brushford Cross*

S.P

| Dulverton | 1903 | 1933 |
|---|---|---|
| Passenger tickets issued | 23330 | 13800 |
| Season Tickets issued | - | 40 |
| Parcels forwarded | 16567 | 16354 |
| General goods forwarded (tons) | 2116 | 1349 |
| Coal and coke received | 1100 | 1098 |
| Other minerals received | 2511 | 1786 |
| General goods received | 7107 | 5106 |
| Trucks of livestock handled | 430 | 275 |

d

The 1905 edition includes the small turntable which was added in the 1880s. More sidings and a loop line for the down platform were brought into use on 6th January 1910. The reservoir was GWR property.

46. The beauty of Exmoor and the fishing have for long attracted visitors and Lord Carnarvon built a hotel (centre) in a strategic position at the station approach. The nearby village was Brushford, Dulverton being 2½ miles to the north and had a population of around 1300 between 1901 and 1961. (Lens of Sutton)

47. The 11.25 am Barnstaple Junction to Taunton calls on 20th August 1953, while the two coaches of an autotrain wait in the loop to return to Exeter. Note the starting signal part way along that platform. (C.L.Caddy coll.)

48. Photographed on the same day was the locomotive of the autotrain and an 0-6-0PT with brake van working a pick-up goods of little revenue value. The passing loop had been extended at its southern end in May 1937. (C.L.Caddy coll.)

49.    The Exe Valley train was formed of conventional coaches when photographed on 25th September 1956. The yard crane was rated at 6-ton capacity and is to be seen on the left. The doorway of the goods shed would have suited broad gauge wagons. (R.M.Casserley)

50.    Here is steam in profusion in a superb setting on 30th July 1963. No. 6327 arrives with the 4.10pm (left) from Barnstaple Junction while no. 7333 approaches with the 4.20pm from Taunton, both being members of the 4300 class. Class 1400 0-4-2T no. 1450 waits to leave for Exeter St. Davids at 5.15pm. (S.P.Derek)

51. Earlier the same day, another 4300 was recorded with the 11.15am from Taunton departing at 12.5pm. Two local firms both ran a small bus between the station and the town. (S.P.Derek)

52. BR class 3 2-6-2T no. 82030 nearly obstructs the signalman's crossing to the tablet exchange on the post at the end of the down platform. The train is the 6.43am from Barnstaple Junction on 15th May 1964. The goods yard closed on 6th July 1964. (C.L.Caddy)

53. Most of the sidings had been lifted by the time this picture was taken on 15th August 1964. The loop platform on the right was not used after April of that year. No. 6345 stands with the 4.3pm from Taunton. The corner was removed from the building on the right some years after the loop was added. The remaining down platform and the signal box were taken out of use on 31st July 1966. (E.Wilmshurst)

54. A few minutes later, the photographer recorded the train in which he was travelling, the 3.50pm from Barnstaple Junction. The locomotive was class 4300 no. 7303. The 53-lever signal box dated from January 1910, the position of its predecessor being shown on the map. (E.Wilmshurst)

55. A DMU stands in the down main platform while class 2251 0-6-0 no. 3205 takes water on 27th March 1965. The special train was the last train to run between Halwill and Torrington and is seen with other motive power in picture no. 102 and again in picture no. 115. The locomotive is preserved on the West Somerset Railway. (S.C.Nash)

56. The finely ornamented cover to the footbridge survived to the end of services. The goods shed and main building were still standing in 1995, the latter in use as hotel staff accommodation. For ten weeks in the Ice Age of early 1963, a helicopter took supplies from the goods yard to cut-off farms and dwellings. (C.L.Caddy)

# EAST ANSTEY

57. A loop for passing was first provided here in 1876, it being lengthened in 1910 and again in 1937 to the length seen here. The population of the nearby village did not rise above 220 during the life of the line. (Lens of Sutton)

| East Anstey | 1903 | 1933 |
|---|---|---|
| Passenger tickets issued | 6807 | 4949 |
| Season Tickets issued | - | 16 |
| Parcels forwarded | 5367 | 1860 |
| General goods forwarded (tons) | 440 | 144 |
| Coal and coke received | 74 | - |
| Other minerals received | 1199 | 436 |
| General goods received | 1789 | 1108 |
| Trucks of livestock handled | 60 | 194 |

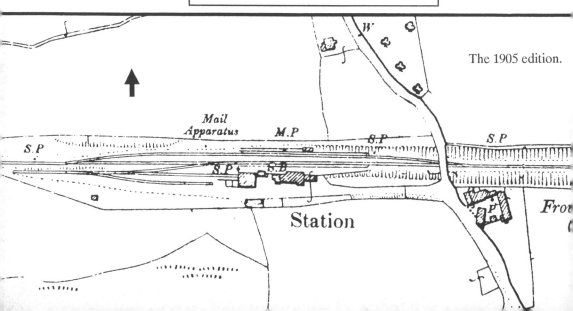

The 1905 edition.

58.	The 4.0pm Barnstaple Junction to Taunton on 5th September 1953 was worked by ex-LSWR class T9 no. 30710. This was a regular Saturday working for this class for several years. (S.C.Nash)

59.	The bridge in the distance is the point at which the line entered Devon for the last time. The signal box was built in 1902 and photographed in 1966. Goods traffic ceased on 30th September 1963; the goods shed and the station were both subsequently converted into dwellings. (C.L.Caddy)

# YEO MILL HALT

60. The halt opened on 27th June 1932 and served only a few dwellings including the quaintly named Ruggleypitt and Cuckoo Farm. Traffic returns were so small that they were included with those of East Anstey.
(Lens of Sutton)

61. The lantern of the previous picture has given way to supports for Tilley lamps. These pressurised burners were a great improvement on a single wick. They were still the responsibility of passing guards.
(Lens of Sutton)

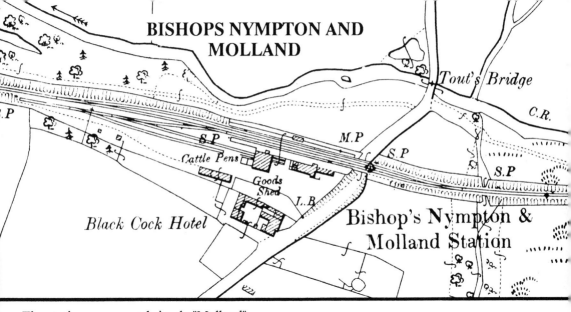

# BISHOPS NYMPTON AND MOLLAND

The station was named simply "Molland" until 1st March 1876. That village was about two miles north-east and had 358 residents in 1901. Bishops Nympton had 893 folk and was almost three miles south-west over a difficult switch-back road. This is the 1904 edition.

62. The 12.44pm from Taunton to Barnstaple Junction arrives behind class 4300 no. 6340 on 6th May 1961 and crosses the bridge which gave road traffic only about nine feet of head-room. Note the catch points in both directions. (E.Wilmshurst)

| Bishop's Nympton and Molland | 1903 | 1933 |
|---|---|---|
| Passenger tickets issued | 7790 | 4875 |
| Season Tickets issued | - | - |
| Parcels forwarded | 4697 | 3151 |
| General goods forwarded (tons) | 477 | 156 |
| Coal and coke received | 76 | 9 |
| Other minerals received | 390 | 675 |
| General goods received | 1687 | 1531 |
| Trucks of livestock handled | 260 | 160 |

63. BR class 3 2-6-2T no. 82040 runs into the up platform, the right hand part of which is on brick arches over a field, as is the waiting shelter. The platform and loop were added in 1876. The loop and up refuge siding were extended in 1937. (C.L.Caddy coll.)

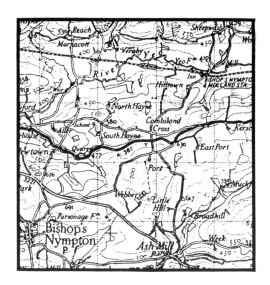

64. The 30-lever signal box dated from 1937 when the passing loop was lengthened. Its predecessor was built in 1902 and was beyond the goods shed. The one before that was at the nearest corner of the goods shed, when the platform ended there. (E.Wilmshurst)

65. The station was photographed just after closure. It was later converted to a private dwelling, as was the goods shed. Goods traffic ceased on 3rd August 1964. (C.L.Caddy)

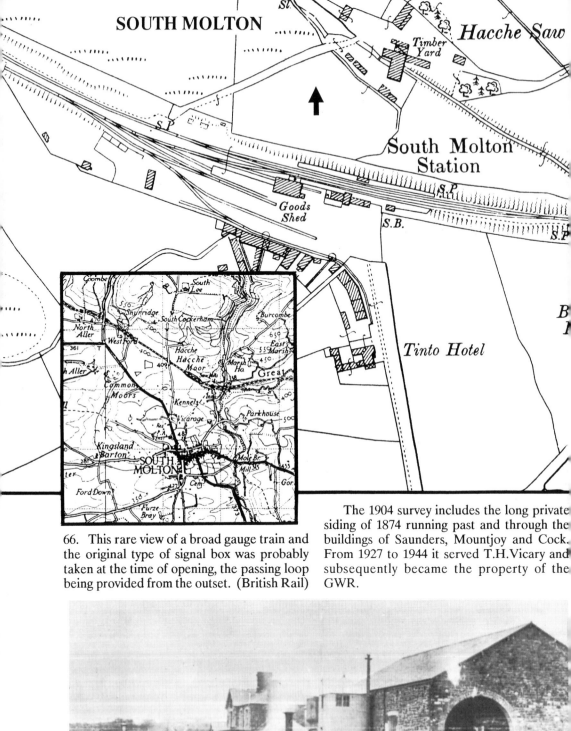

# SOUTH MOLTON

Hacche Saw

Timber Yard

South Molton Station

Goods Shed

S.B.

Tinto Hotel

*Coombe* *South Lee* *Burcombe* *Snydridge* *South Cockerham* *North Aller* *West Ford* *361* *Hacche* *Hacche Moor* *East Marsh* *h Aller* *Common Moors* *Kennels* *Great* *Vicarage* *Parkhouse* *Kingsland Barton* *SOUTH MOLTON* *Mole Br* *Mill* *ter* *Cem* *Gor* *Ford Down* *Furze Bray*

66. This rare view of a broad gauge train and the original type of signal box was probably taken at the time of opening, the passing loop being provided from the outset. (British Rail)

The 1904 survey includes the long private siding of 1874 running past and through the buildings of Saunders, Mountjoy and Cock. From 1927 to 1944 it served T.H. Vicary and subsequently became the property of the GWR.

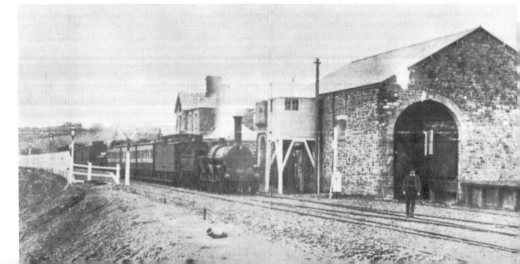

57. With over 2000 inhabitants, the monthly Great Market and biennial sheep fairs, the town was a good source of revenue for the railway, although the town centre was nearly one mile to the south. Passenger trains carried much local produce, as witnessed here. (Lens of Sutton)

58. The white bands on the cattle wagons resulted from the liberal application of limewash in the interests of hygiene. By 1938, the goods yard had a 5-ton capacity crane, the largest at any intermediate station on the route. (Lens of Sutton)

| South Molton | 1903 | 1933 |
|---|---|---|
| Passenger tickets issued | 24099 | 8978 |
| Season Tickets issued | - | 14 |
| Parcels forwarded | 21736 | 20397 |
| General goods forwarded (tons) | 2341 | 1150 |
| Coal and coke received | 1867 | 559 |
| Other minerals received | 2573 | 4497 |
| General goods received | 6718 | 8443 |
| Trucks of livestock handled | 579 | 210 |

69. The 33-lever signal box replaced the one seen in picture no. 66 in about 1901. Extreme care had to be taken here and at other stations on the route that were on a gradient. Every wagon had to have its brake applied and sprags had to be kept at intervals in the 6ft. between the tracks. Some are visible. Ironstone was once mined locally. The Florence Mining Company had a siding on the north side of the line about ½ mile east of the station from 1882 to about 1893. There was a tramway between the siding and the mine. (Lens of Sutton)

70. Mail bags and general merchandise await an up train as class 4300 no. 6372 also awaits its arrival in April 1963. For many years, the luncheon car from Paddington was shunted here from the down train to an up service. (C.L.Caddy coll.)

71. The down platform was signalled for the passage of up trains from 2nd May 1928. The 11.5am Ilfracombe to Wolverhampton Low Level is proceeding thus on 17th August 1963. The arrangement would have facilitated parcel loading. (S.P.Derek)

72. The loop was extended in 1907, as were the platforms. This timber part was barricaded off by 1963 on safety grounds. No. 82040 was one of the BR standard class 3 2-6-2s which partially superseded the ageing 4300s. (C.L.Caddy coll.)

73. As elsewhere, the loop was further increased in length in 1937. Photographed in decline in 1966, the station had been the starting point for rabbit specials in the 1930s. In the 1940s there were three goods trains each weekday, two calling here. (C.L.Caddy)

74. Goods services were withdrawn on 3rd August 1964, by which time there were such trains on alternate days only. A 1992 photograph reveals that the main buildings were still in situ. The goods shed was also standing. The A461(T) now runs on the other side of the building and on the entire length of the trackbed from here to Barnstaple, obliterating all traces of former railway occupation. (D.Dornom)

# EAST OF FILLEIGH

August 1926

**LONDON, TAUNTON, DULVERTON, BARNSTAPLE, and ILFRACOMBE.—Great Western.**

| Miles | Down. | Week Days only. ngt. | mrn | mrn | mrn S | mrn | | aft | | aft | aft | aft S | | |
|---|---|---|---|---|---|---|---|---|---|---|---|---|---|---|
| | 12London (Pad.) ....dep. | 12b0 | 5 30 | .... | 9 0 | 10K30 | .... | 1 30 | Through Carriage, London (Pad.) to Ilfracombe. | .... | 4 30 | 6 30 | .... | .... |
| — | Taunton ............dep. | 8 0 | 1030 | .... | 1225 | 1 15 | .... | 4 35 | | 5 20 | 8 10 | 1115 | .... | .... |
| 2 | Norton Fitzwarren ...... | 8 4 | 1037 | .... | .... | 1 19 | .... | .... | | 5 24 | 8 14 | 1120 | .... | .... |
| 6¼ | Milverton ............... | 8 13 | 1046 | .... | 1239 | 1 28 | .... | .... | | 5 35 | 8 23 | 1130 | .... | .... |
| 9¼ | Wiveliscombe ........... | 8 22 | 1052 | .... | 1246 | 1 35 | .... | .... | | 5 42 | 8 30 | 1137 | .... | .... |
| 14¼ | Venn Cross .............. | 8 33 | 11 3 | .... | .... | 1 46 | .... | .... | | 5 53 | 8 41 | .... | .... | .... |
| 17¾ | Morebath.................. | 8 42 | 1112 | .... | .... | 1 54 | .... | .... | | 6 1 | 8 49 | .... | .... | .... |
| 21 | Dulverton 57 ........... | 8 50 | 1118 | 1132 | 1 12 | 2 5 | .... | 5 13 | | 6 10 | 8 58 | .... | .... | .... |
| 24¾ | East Anstey ....[Molland | 8 58 | .... | 1142 | .... | 2 14 | .... | .... | | 6 19 | 9 7 | .... | .... | .... |
| 30 | Bishop's Nympton and | 9 8 | .... | 1151 | .... | 2 23 | .... | .... | | 6 28 | 9 16 | .... | .... | .... |
| 34¼ | South Molton............ | 9 18 | .... | 12 1 | 1 40 | 2 33 | .... | 5 35 | | 6 40 | 9 25 | .... | .... | .... |
| 37¼ | Filleigh ................... | 9 26 | .... | 12 9 | .... | 2 41 | .... | .... | | 6 48 | 9 33 | .... | .... | .... |
| 41 | Swimbridge... ........... | 9 35 | .... | 1218 | .... | 2 53 | .... | .... | | 6 57 | 9 42 | .... | .... | .... |
| 44¾ | Barnstaple .... arr. | 9 41 | .... | 1224 | 2 0 | 2 59 | .... | 5 53 | | 7 3 | 9 48 | .... | .... | .... |
| | (G W.) A 176... dep. | 9 55 | .... | 1235 | 2 15 | 3 10 | .... | 6 1 | | 7 25 | .... | .... | .... | .... |
| 45¾ | Barnstaple J. 176...arr. | 10 0 | .... | 1240 | 2 20 | 3 15 | .... | 6 6 | | 7 30 | .... | .... | .... | .... |
| 60¾ | Ilfracombe 176...... " | 11 8 | .... | 2 0 | 3 12 | 4 24 | .... | 7 3 | | 8 27 | .... | .... | .... | .... |

| Miles | Up. | Week Days only. mrn | mrn | mrn | | aft | aft | aft | | | |
|---|---|---|---|---|---|---|---|---|---|---|---|
| | Ilfracombe ..........dep. | .... | .... | 9 55 | .... | 1 30 | 2 50 | 4 35 | .... | .... | .... |
| 15 | Barnstaple Jun. .... " | .... | .... | 10 44 | .... | 2 30 | 3 47 | 5 35 | .... | .... | .... |
| 16 | Barnstaple arr. | .... | .... | 10 49 | .... | 2 35 | 3 52 | 5 40 | .... | .... | .... |
| | (G.W.) A .... dep. | 7 5 | 8 50 | 10 58 | .... | 2 40 | 4 0 | 6 10 | .... | .... | .... |
| 19¾ | Swimbridge............... | 7 13 | 8 59 | 11 6 | .... | .... | 4 8 | 6 20 | .... | .... | .... |
| 23½ | Filleigh .................... | 7 21 | 9 7 | 11 14 | .... | .... | 4 16 | 6 30 | .... | .... | .... |
| 26½ | South Molton ...[Molland | 7 30 | 9 17 | 11 24 | .... | .... | 4 26 | 6 45 | .... | .... | .... |
| 30¾ | Bishop's Nympton and | 7 38 | 9 25 | 11 32 | .... | .... | 4 35 | 6 55 | .... | .... | .... |
| 36 | East Anstey ............ | 7 46 | 9 33 | 11 41 | .... | .... | 4 44 | 7 5 | .... | .... | .... |
| 39½ | Dulverton 57............ | 7 54 | 9 41 | 11 50 | .... | 3 25 | 4 55 | 7 16 | .... | .... | .... |
| 43 | Morebath.................. | 8 4 | 9 51 | 12 0 | .... | .... | 5 6 | 7 27 | .... | .... | .... |
| 46½ | Venn Cross ............... | 8 12 | 9 59 | 12 8 | .... | .... | 5 14 | 7 37 | .... | .... | .... |
| 51½ | Wiveliscombe ........... | 8 23 | 10 8 | 12 17 | .... | .... | 5 25 | 7 47 | .... | .... | .... |
| 54½ | Milverton ................. | 8 29 | 1014 | 12 23 | .... | .... | 5 34 | 7 55 | .... | .... | .... |
| 58½ | Norton Fitzwarren 22 ... | 8 41 | 1022 | .... | .... | .... | 5 42 | 8 3 | .... | .... | .... |
| 60¾ | Taunton 7, 17, 22 ....arr | 8 45 | 1026 | 12 34 | .... | 4 0 | 5 46 | 8 7 | .... | .... | .... |
| 203¾ | 17London (Pad.).... arr. | .... | 1 15 | 4 5 | .... | 6 50 | 9 0 | 2 40 | .... | .... | .... |

**A** Over ¾ mile to Barnstaple Town Station. *b* Departs Paddington at 9 50 aft. on Sundays.
**K** Slip Carriage. **S** Saturdays only.

75. Filleigh Viaduct was 321yds in length and had six spans, with a maximum height of 94ft, passing over the River Bray. Class N 2-6-0 no. 31843 is working the 4.0pm Barnstaple Junction to Taunton on 4th September 1953. This was a normal Monday - Friday duty for this class. Motorists now cross the valley encased by the high concrete walls of a new bridge. (S.C.Nash)

76. East of the viaduct was the 319yd long Castle Hill Tunnel. It is seen from an up train in 1956 and was eliminated by a deep cutting by the road builders of the late 1980s. (H.C.Casserley)

# FILLEIGH

Filleigh Station

Post Office

Guide Po.

Signal Post

*Filleigh Brid*

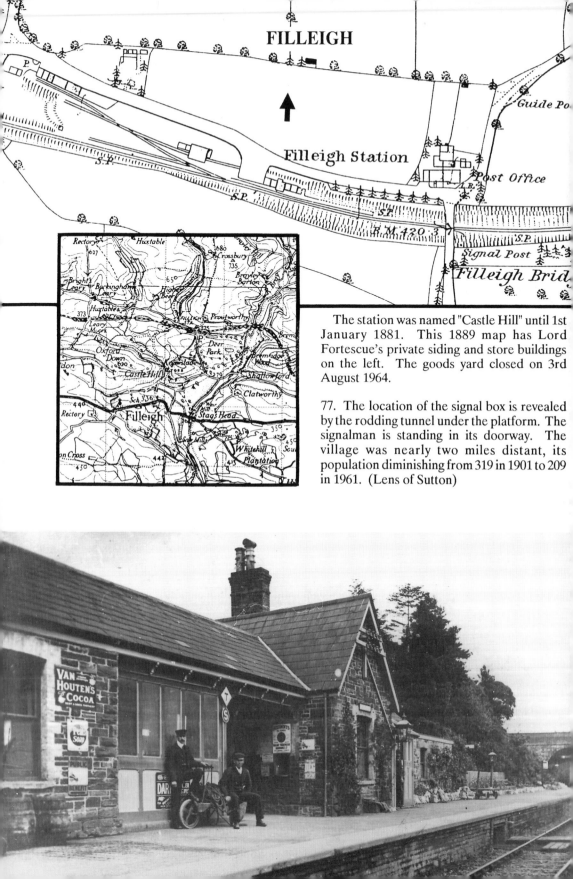

The station was named "Castle Hill" until 1st January 1881. This 1889 map has Lord Fortescue's private siding and store buildings on the left. The goods yard closed on 3rd August 1964.

77. The location of the signal box is revealed by the rodding tunnel under the platform. The signalman is standing in its doorway. The village was nearly two miles distant, its population diminishing from 319 in 1901 to 209 in 1961. (Lens of Sutton)

78. A new 42-lever signal box was opened on 20th June 1937, when a loop was provided for the first time. Beyond it, another loop was completed on 15th December 1937, but it was on the up side and was for goods traffic. The middle signal gave down trains access to it. This loop was taken out of use on 20th December 1961 and the other followed on 6th September 1964 when the box also closed. (Lens of Sutton)

79. The goods loop is evident in the distance as the signalman offers the token to the driver of class 4300 no. 6350 on 17th August 1963. The train is the 12.25 (Saturdays only) Ilfracombe to Taunton which omitted this and four other stops on the route. The remote points were electricially operated. (S.P.Derek)

| Filleigh | 1903 | 1933 |
|---|---|---|
| Passenger tickets issued | 8200 | 4555 |
| Season Tickets issued | - | 2 |
| Parcels forwarded | 2729 | 2810 |
| General goods forwarded (tons) | 358 | 1167 |
| Coal and coke received | 823 | 113 |
| Other minerals received | 380 | 402 |
| General goods received | 1350 | 1623 |
| Trucks of livestock handled | 127 | 66 |

# SWIMBRIDGE

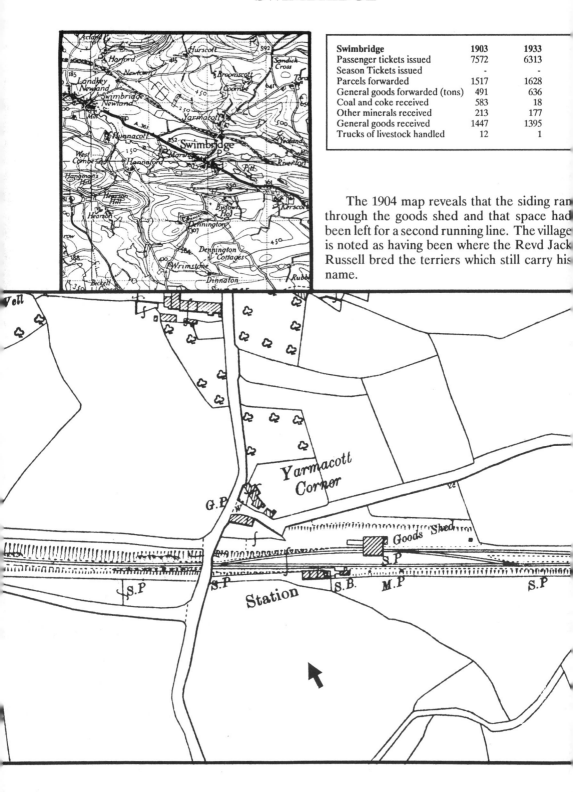

| Swimbridge | 1903 | 1933 |
|---|---|---|
| Passenger tickets issued | 7572 | 6313 |
| Season Tickets issued | - | - |
| Parcels forwarded | 1517 | 1628 |
| General goods forwarded (tons) | 491 | 636 |
| Coal and coke received | 583 | 18 |
| Other minerals received | 213 | 177 |
| General goods received | 1447 | 1395 |
| Trucks of livestock handled | 12 | 1 |

The 1904 map reveals that the siding ran through the goods shed and that space had been left for a second running line. The village is noted as having been where the Revd Jack Russell bred the terriers which still carry his name.

80. The down platform (right) was the only one until the loop was brought into use on 24th February 1904. The village was close by and had about 1000 residents. (Lens of Sutton)

81. No. 6372 is hauling the 2.24pm Barnstaple Junction to Taunton on 15th April 1963 and is seen from the 1.3pm from Taunton which was headed by no. 6327. (S.P.Derek)

82. This signal box was commissioned on 6th April 1937, when the extended loop was brought into use. Class 4300 no. 6372 pauses in the evening sun in April 1963. (C.L.Caddy coll.)

83. The goods yard closed on 3rd August 1964 but the station and loop remained in use to the end. (Lens of Sutton)

# BARNSTAPLE EAST LOOP

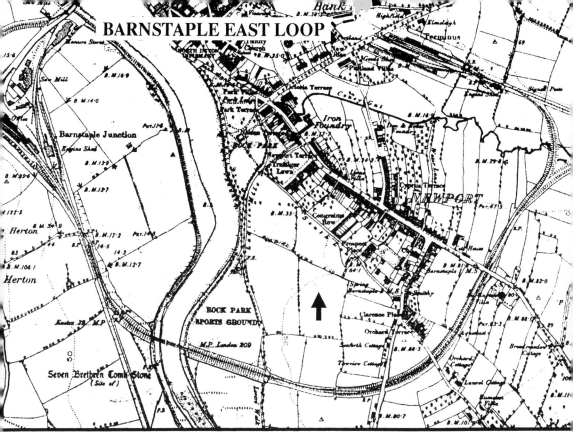

The 1890 edition at 6" to 1 mile has Barnstaple Junction on the left, the LSWR line from Exeter at the bottom and the GWR terminus top right. Barnstaple East Junction is just off the right border while Barnstaple South Junction is at the bottom of the triangle. "Junction" was replaced by the word "Loop" on 11th March 1950.

84. The Royal Train approaches East Loop on 8th May 1956, hauled by unusually clean locomotives, nos. 6372 and 6385. The occupants proceeded on a tour of Devon by road and rejoined the train at Launceston. (S.C.Nash)

85. The East Curve opened on 1st July 1905 and was used in most summers until 4th September 1939. It reopened on 12th June 1960 when the points and the direct line (left) to the terminus at Victoria Road were removed. New flat bottom rails lie ready to be installed. (J.J.Smith)

# BARNSTAPLE WEST LOOP

86. Approaching Victoria Road on 3rd June 1960 is no. 6337 with the 5.45pm from Taunton. The signal on the right is on the West Loop. Prior to 1940, some Ilfracombe-bound trains stopped just beyond South Junction and detached one or two coaches which were hauled back to the terminus. In the reverse direction, coaches were propelled to East Junction for attachment. (S.C.Nash)

87. Pictured leaving Victoria Road on the same day is no. 7304. These two signals are on the right of the previous picture. This junction ceased to function on 12th June 1960 when the station closed to passengers. (S.C.Nash)

88. No. 6390 is rounding West Loop on 11th June 1960 with the 3.58pm Barnstaple Junction to Taunton. The locomotive would run round at Victoria Road and be chimney first for the remainder of the 46 mile journey. South Loop Box was reduced to a ground frame on 12th June 1960 and was taken out of use on 3rd October 1966. (J.J.Smith)

| Miles | | MONDAYS TO FRIDAYS | | | | | | | |
|---|---|---|---|---|---|---|---|---|---|
| | | am | am | am | | pm | pm | pm G | pm F |
| | 62 London (Pad.) 61 dep | .. | 8 30 | 10 30 | .. | 12 30 | 2 30 | 4 30 | 6 30 |
| — | **Taunton** dep | 8 5 | 11 15 | pm 1 15 | .. | 4 20 | 5 55 | 7 15 | 9 10 |
| 6½ | Milverton | 8 17 | 11 29 | 1 28 | .... | 4 32 | 6 7 | 7 26 | 9 21 |
| 9½ | Wiveliscombe | 8 25 | 11 37 | 1 35 | .. | 4 39 | 6 15 | 7 33 | 9 28 |
| 14¼ | Venn Cross | 8 36 | 11 48 | 1 46 | .... | 4 51 | 6 26 | 7 44 | 9 39 |
| 17¾ | Morebath | 8 42 | 11 54 | 1 52 | .. | 4 57 | 6 32 | 7 50 | 9 45 |
| 19¼ | Morebath Junction Halt | 8 47 | 11 59 | 1 57 | .... | 5 2 | 6 37 | 7 58 | 9 49 |
| 21 | Dulverton | 8 53 | 12 5 | 2 5 | .. | 5 10 | 6 44 | 8 4 | 9 55 |
| 24¾ | East Anstey | 9 3 | 12 14 | 2 14 | .... | 5 19 | 6 53 | 8 13 | 10 4 |
| 26½ | Yeo Mill Halt | 9 8 | 12 19 | 2 19 | .. | 5 24 | 6 58 | 8 18 | 10 9 |
| 30 | Bishop's Nympton and | 9 14 | 12 25 | 2 25 | .... | 5 30 | 7 4 | 8 24 | 10 15 |
| 34¼ | South Molton .[Molland | 9 23 | 12 33 | 2 33 | .. | 5 39 | 7 14 | 8 32 | 10 23 |
| 37¼ | Filleigh | 9 32 | 12 42 | 2 45 | .... | 5 48 | 7 23 | 8 41 | 10 32 |
| 40¾ | Swimbridge | 9 39 | 12 49 | 2 52 | .. | 5 55 | 7 30 | 8 48 | 10 39 |
| 45¾ | **Barnstaple Junction** arr | 9 49 | 12 59 | 3 2 | .... | 6 5 | 7 40 | 8 58 | 10 49 |
| 60¾ | **Ilfracombe** arr | 10 48 | 1 44 | 3 51 | .. | 7 2 | 9 2 | .. | .. |

| Miles | | SATURDAYS | | | | | | | | | | | |
|---|---|---|---|---|---|---|---|---|---|---|---|---|---|
| | | am T | am T | am T | am | pm W | am T | | pm | | pm | pm | |
| | 62 London (Pad.) 61 dep | .. | .. | .. | 8 1[illegible] | .. | 10 15 | .. | 12 30 | .. | 2 30 | 6 30 | .. |
| — | **Taunton** dep | 6 20 | 7 0 | 8 50 | 11 2[illegible] | 1 5 | pm 1 57 | .. | 4 25 | .. | 5 55 | 9 10 | .. |
| 6½ | Milverton | .... | 7 12 | 9 2 | 11 37 | 1 23 | 2 9 | .... | 4 37 | .... | 6 7 | 9 21 | .... |
| 9½ | Wiveliscombe | 6 39 | 7 19 | 9 10 | 11 44 | 1 31 | 2 17 | .. | 4 45 | .. | 6 15 | 9 28 | .. |
| 14¼ | Venn Cross | .... | 7 30 | 9 21 | 11 55 | .... | .... | .... | 4 56 | .... | 6 26 | 9 39 | .... |
| 17¾ | Morebath | .. | 7 36 | 9 27 | 12 1 | .. | .. | .. | 5 2 | .. | 6 32 | 9 45 | .. |
| 19¼ | Morebath Junction Halt | .... | .... | 9 32 | 12 6 | .... | .... | .... | 5 7 | .... | 6 37 | 9 49 | .... |
| 21 | Dulverton | 7 6 | 7 48 | 9 38 | 12 12 | 2 8 | 2 50 | .. | 5 13 | .. | 6 44 | 9 55 | .. |
| 24¾ | East Anstey | .... | 7 58 | 9 48 | 12 21 | .... | 3 1 | .... | 5 22 | .... | 6 53 | 10 4 | .... |
| 26½ | Yeo Mill Halt | .. | .. | 9 53 | 12 26 | .. | .. | .. | 5 27 | .. | 6 58 | 10 9 | .. |
| 30 | Bishop's Nympton and | 7 26 | 8 8 | 10 0 | 12 34 | .... | 3 13 | .... | 5 33 | .... | 7 4 | 10 15 | .... |
| 34¼ | South Molton .[Molland | 7 38 | 8 18 | 10 13 | 12 43 | 2 36 | 3 23 | .. | 5 42 | .. | 7 14 | 10 23 | .. |
| 37¼ | Filleigh | 7 48 | 8 28 | 10 24 | 12 52 | .... | 3 32 | .... | 5 51 | .... | 7 23 | 10 32 | .... |
| 40¾ | Swimbridge | 7 58 | 8 35 | 10 31 | 12 59 | .. | 3 41 | .. | 5 58 | .. | 7 30 | 10 39 | .. |
| 45¾ | **Barnstaple Junction** arr | 8 8 | 8 45 | 10 43 | 1 11 | 3 2 | 3 53 | .... | 6 8 | .... | 7 43 | 10 49 | .... |
| 60¾ | **Ilfracombe** arr | 9 4 | 9 42 | 11 28 | 2 41 | 4 0 | 4 53 | .. | 7 2 | .. | 9 2 | .. | .. |

| Miles | | MONDAYS TO FRIDAYS | | | | | | | | |
|---|---|---|---|---|---|---|---|---|---|---|
| | | am | am | am | | pm | pm | | pm | |
| — | **Ilfracombe** dep | .. | 6 48 | 8 55 | .. | 12 15 | 3 0 | . | 5 57 | .. |
| 15 | **Barnstaple Junction** dep | 6 43 | 8 12 | 10 50 | .... | 2 24 | 4 10 | ... | 6 47 | .... |
| 20 | Swimbridge | 6 53 | 8 22 | 11 0 | .. | 2 36 | 4 20 | . | 6 57 | .. |
| 23½ | Filleigh | 7 1 | 8 30 | 11 8 | .... | 2 44 | 4 28 | ... | 7 5 | .... |
| 26½ | South Molton .[Molland | 7 13 | 8 42 | 11 20 | .. | 2 56 | 4 40 | . | 7 17 | .. |
| 30¾ | Bishop's Nympton and | 7 21 | 8 50 | 11 28 | .... | 3 4 | 4 48 | ... | 7 25 | .... |
| 34¼ | Yeo Mill Halt | 7 28 | 8 57 | 11 35 | .. | 3 11 | 4 55 | . | 7 32 | .. |
| 36 | East Anstey | 7 33 | 9 4 | 11 40 | .... | 3 16 | 5 0 | ... | 7 37 | .... |
| 39¾ | Dulverton | 7 43 | 9 15 | 11 49 | .. | 3 25 | 5 9 | . | 7 47 | .. |
| 41½ | Morebath Junction Halt | 7 48 | 9 21 | 11 54 | .... | 3 30 | 5 14 | ... | 7 52 | .... |
| 43 | Morebath | 7 51 | 9 24 | 12 3 | .. | 3 34 | 5 18 | . | 7 56 | .. |
| 46½ | Venn Cross | 7 59 | 9 32 | 12 11 | .... | 3 41 | 5 25 | ... | 8 4 | .... |
| 51¼ | Wiveliscombe | 8 9 | 9 41 | 12 20 | .. | 3 52 | 5 35 | . | 8 14 | .. |
| 54¼ | Milverton | 8 15 | 9 47 | 12 26 | .... | 3 58 | 5 41 | ... | 8 21 | .... |
| 60¾ | **Taunton** arr | 8 27 | 9 59 | 12 40 | .. | 4 14 | 5 56 | . | 8 34 | .. |
| 203¾ | 62 London (Pad.) 61 arr | 11 15 | pm 1 20 | pm 3 25 | .. | 7 20 | 9 13 | . | .. | .. |

| Miles | | SATURDAYS | | | | | | | | | | |
|---|---|---|---|---|---|---|---|---|---|---|---|---|
| | | am | | am M | am T | am C | am W | | pm T | pm | pm T | pm T |
| — | **Ilfracombe** dep | .. | .. | 8 35 | 9 20 | 10 10 | 11 5 | .. | 12 25 | 2 55 | 5 57 | 6 37 |
| 15 | **Barnstaple Junction** dep | 6 45 | .... | 9 23 | 10 3 | 11 5 | 11 58 | .... | 1 11 | 3 55 | 6 47 | 7 18 |
| 20 | Swimbridge | 6 57 | .. | .. | .. | 11 19 | .. | .. | .. | 4 8 | 6 57 | 7 32 |
| 23½ | Filleigh | 7 5 | .... | .... | .... | 11 27 | .... | .... | .... | 4 16 | 7 5 | 7 40 |
| 26½ | South Molton .[Molland | 7 16 | .. | 9 54 | 10 31 | 11 38 | 12 26 | .. | 1 39 | 4 27 | 7 17 | 7 51 |
| 30¾ | Bishop's Nympton and | 7 25 | .... | .... | .... | 11 47 | .... | .... | 1 47 | 4 36 | 7 25 | 8 1 |
| 34¼ | Yeo Mill Halt | 7 32 | .. | .. | .. | 11 54 | .. | .. | .. | 4 43 | 7 32 | 8 8 |
| 36 | East Anstey | 7 37 | .... | .... | .... | 12 0 | .... | .... | 2 0 | 4 48 | 7 37 | 8 13 |
| 39¾ | Dulverton | 7 47 | .. | 10 22 | 10 58 | 12 10 | 12 52 | .. | 2 10 | 4 59 | 7 47 | 8 24 |
| 41½ | Morebath Junction Halt | 7 53 | .... | .... | .... | 12 16 | .... | .... | .... | 5 4 | 7 52 | 8 29 |
| 43 | Morebath | 7 56 | .. | .. | .. | 12 20 | .. | .. | .. | 5 11 | 7 56 | 8 33 |
| 46½ | Venn Cross | 8 4 | .... | .... | .... | 12 28 | .... | .... | 2 28 | 5 19 | 8 4 | 8 41 |
| 51¼ | Wiveliscombe | 8 14 | .. | 10 49 | 11 24 | 12 39 | 1 18 | .. | 2 39 | 5 30 | 8 14 | 8 51 |
| 54¼ | Milverton | 8 20 | .... | .... | .... | 12 45 | .... | .... | 2 45 | 5 36 | 8 21 | 8 57 |
| 60¾ | **Taunton** arr | 8 32 | .. | 11 5 | 11 41 | 1 0 | 1 35 | .. | 2 57 | 5 48 | 8 34 | 9 10 |
| 203¾ | 62 London (Pad.) 61 arr | 11 33 | .. | .. | pm 3 12 | .. | 4 32 | .. | 6 36 | 9 3 | .. | .. |

**C** Through Train between Ilfracombe and Cardiff (Table 61)
**F** Fridays only
**G** Mondays to Thursdays only
**M** Through Train Ilfracombe to Bristol. Commencing 29th June extended to Manchester (Ex.) (Tables 61 and 168)
**T** Through Train between Taunton and Ilfracombe
**W** Through Train between Wolverhampton (L.L.) and Ilfracombe

Summer 1963

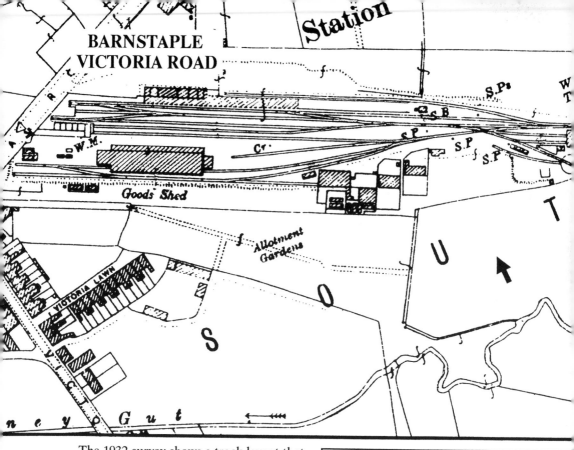

BARNSTAPLE
VICTORIA ROAD

The 1932 survey shows a track layout that had changed very little since the first edition.

89. This view from the end loading dock must be before 1925 as the crossover on the right had been lifted by that time. The cylinders contain gas for the restaurant cars. (Lens of Sutton)

| Barnstaple | 1903 | 1933 |
|---|---|---|
| Passenger tickets issued | 32987 | 15715 |
| Season Tickets issued | - | 78 |
| Parcels forwarded | 34046 | 64111 |
| General goods forwarded (tons) | 6369 | 3717 |
| Coal and coke received | 877 | 216 |
| Other minerals received | 3113 | 2848 |
| General goods received | 11290 | 23562 |
| Trucks of livestock handled | 576 | 166 |

90. Another pre-1925 photograph shows more period rolling stock and also detail of the gas lamps. The GWR for long favoured clerestorey coaches of the type seen in the siding along with a cattle truck and horse box. (Lens of Sutton)

91. The initial temporary station was replaced by this timber building in 1876. For many years, a horse bus conveyed passengers to Barnstaple Junction. (British Rail)

92. A picture from 1928 illustrates a locomotive type not seen previously on the branch. No. 3335 *Tregothnan* was of the "Bulldog" class. This type with curved frames was introduced in 1898.
(Rev.N.Pocock/F.Hornby coll.)

93. Seen in 1933 is another "Bulldog", no. 3416 *John.W.Wilson*. This is of the straight frame type. The outside coupling rods made a fascinating functioning feature and a satisfactory seat for shunters.
(J.W.Wilson/R.S.Carpenter coll.)

94. Trains often passed at this station. No. 6343 is waiting to leave for Barnstaple Junction at 4.10pm on 28th September 1956, having arrived at the other platform, run round and shunted to the bay. (H.C.Casserley)

95. Photographed a few minutes later is no. 6390, with the 3.58 from Barnstaple Junction which arrived at 4.3 and departed for Taunton at 4.12. No wonder that officials were keen to eliminate these slow and wasteful procedures. (H.C.Casserley)

96. The suffix "Victoria Road" was added to the station name on 26th September 1949 but the S&T Dept. did not adopt it until 11th March 1950. The box and water tank were recorded in September 1956. Signalling ceased at the end of passenger services. (H.C.Casserley)

97. The 4.35pm Taunton to Barnstaple Junction was hauled by no. 6309 on 3rd June 1960. The train was booked here from 6.16 to 6.24, but it did not pass another here. (S.C.Nash)

98. No. 7304 reverses in with the 6.40pm Barnstaple Junction to Taunton later the same day, with a diverse range of vans. This was the last up train of the day. The last down train terminated here at 10.6pm. (S.C.Nash)

# DEVON and SOMERSET.—Great Western,

| Down. | | | Week Days. | | | | | | | Sundays | |
|---|---|---|---|---|---|---|---|---|---|---|---|
| Paddington Station, | mrn | mrn | mrn | mrn | mrn | aft | | | | mrn | mrn |
|   LONDON 2......dep | .... | 5 30 | 9 0 | 1145 | 1030 | 5 0 | .... | .... | .... | .... | 10 0 | .... |
|   BRISTOL 3...... ,, | 6 15 | 9 10 | 1210 | 2 26 | 3 15 | 8 15 | .... | .... | .... | 6 30 | 3 30 | .... |
|   EXETER 6 ...... ,, | 6 0 | 9 45 | 1250 | .... | 4 45 | 5 50 | .... | .... | .... | .... | 3 25 | .... |
| **Down.** | 1,2,3 | 1,2,3 | 1,2,3 | 1,2,3 | 1,2,3 | gov | | | | gov | 1,2,3 | |
| Taunton ..........dep | 7 55 | 1110 | 1 40 | 3 40 | 5 55 | 9 40 | .... | .... | .... | 8 30 | 5 35 | .... |
| Norton Fitzwarren.... | 8 0 | 1116 | 1 45 | 3 46 | 6 1 | 9 45 | .... | .... | .... | 8 36 | 5 45 | .... |
| Milverton ........... | 8 9 | 1126 | 1 55 | 3 56 | 6 12 | 9 51 | .... | .... | .... | 8 46 | 5 51 | .... |
| Wiveliscombe ....... | 8 18 | 1136 | 2 5 | 4 6 | 6 23 | 10 3 | .... | .... | .... | 8 56 | 6 1 | .... |
| Venn Cross........... | 8 30 | 1148 | 2 16 | Sat. | 6 37 | .... | .... | .... | .... | 9 8 | 6 13 | .... |
| Morebath, for Bampton | 8 40 | 1157 | 3 25 | 4 32 | 6 46 | 1022 | .... | .... | .... | 9 17 | 6 2 | |
| Dulverton ........... | 8 50 | 12 7 | 2 33 | 4 42 | 7 0 | 1035 | .... | .... | .... | 9 27 | 6 32 | .... |
| East Anstey..[Molland | 9 8 | 1224 | .... | 4 54 | 7 12 | .... | .... | .... | .... | 9 40 | 6 45 | .... |
| Bishop's Nympton and | 9 32 | 1230 | .... | 5 6 | 7 24 | .... | .... | .... | .... | 9 51 | 6 56 | .... |
| South Molton ....... | 9 45 | 1244 | 3 57 | 5 21 | 7 39 | 1455 | .... | .... | .... | 10 4 | 7 9 | .... |
| Castle Hill .......... | 9 56 | 1254 | 3 6 | 5 30 | 7 47 | 11 5 | .... | .... | .... | 1014 | 7 19 | .... |
| Swimbridge ......... | 10 51 | 8 | 3 15 | .... | 7 57 | .... | .... | .... | .... | 1023 | 7 28 | .... |
| Barnstaple ... arr | 1016 | 1 15 | 3 26 | 5 45 | 8 10 | 1124 | .... | .... | .... | 1 35 | 7 40 | .... |
| Ilfracombe (Coach) ,, | .... | 3 15 | 5 25 | 7 40 | .... | .... | .... | .... | .... | .... | .... | .... |

July 1878

99. A turntable 42 ft. in length and a two-road engine shed had been in use on the land on the left until 1st January 1951. The southernmost siding served a petrol store at its eastern end. This is the last day of passenger services, 11th June 1960. (J.J.Smith)

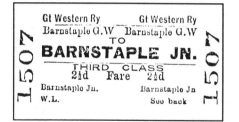

100. The signals and nameboards soon disappeared but the goods depot remained busy, being worked as a siding from Barnstaple Junction. The jib of the 6-ton crane is visible in this late June 1960 view. (N.L.Browne)

101. The curved extension to the original platform canopy was walled in to form a store. The still unbroken gas lamps and the loading gauge are also visible. All parcel traffic was concentrated here in 1948, such service ceasing at the other two Barnstaple stations. (Lens of Sutton)

102. The "Exmoor Ranger" on 27th March 1965 ran into the goods yard from Halwill before doing a return trip to Ilfracombe and then running on to Taunton. The special started and terminated at Exeter St. Davids. The train engine is no. 41206. (S.C.Nash)

103. The sidings were named middle, cattle, carriage, mileage, short, shed and back. The petrol siding branched from the latter. The goods depot closed on 5th March 1970, after which date all traffic was concentrated at Barnstaple Junction. (Lens of Sutton)

104. A 1992 photograph from the road that was built on the site of the platforms shows the goods shed for sale. It became the Grosvenor Church and was fitted with a spirelet and cross, an apt use if you accept the explanation of GWR used on the back cover. (D.Dornom)

# EAST OF BARNSTAPLE JUNCTION

105. The 1905 connecting spur between the GWR and LSWR passed over the River Taw on a five span bridge 119yds in length. No. 5336 is crossing it on 15th August 1964 with the 10.17am Cardiff General to Ilfracombe. (E.Wilmshurst)

106. Approaching the bridge on 28th September 1956 is no. 6390 with the 3.58pm from Barnstaple Junction to Taunton. The bridge is now crossed by the Tarka Trail, part of an extensive series of foot and cycle ways in North Devon. (H.C.Casserley)

107. The Taw Bridge is in the background as N class 2-6-0 no. 31849 approaches Barnstaple Junction with a train from Taunton on 29th June 1960. The final length of the GWR spur ran parallel to the LSWR double track for about 100yds; the rear coach has just left the spur. (S.C.Nash)

08. The first platform was the one on the right up), a second was added in 1874 and in 1924 he hill was cut back to provide a third. Note hat there were four tracks through part of the tation. (Lens of Sutton)

109. We witness lunchtime activity on 5th August 1939. Class 4500 2-6-2T no. 5542 arrived at 1.38pm with a train from Taunton that included a clerestorey coach. The train on the left is the 1.20pm from Ilfracombe and is being divided. Class N no. 1858 will take the front portion on to Yeoford, while the rear part will run on the GWR route. (J.R.W.Kirkby)

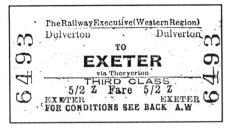

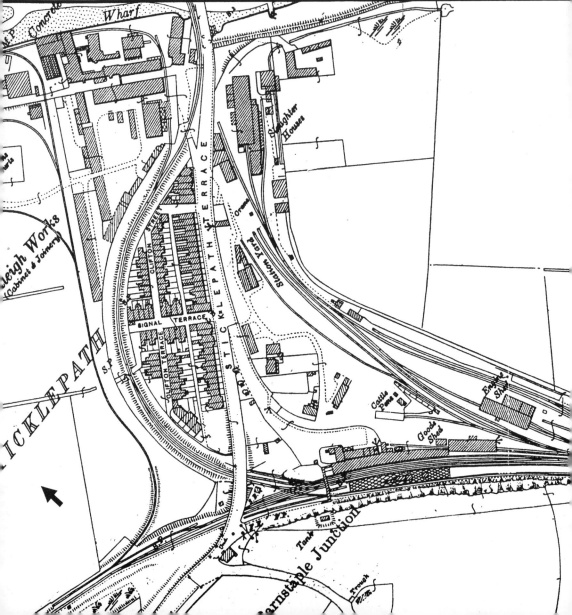

110. Only partially cleaned, no. 6323 waits to depart for Taunton in 1950, with its tank lid open. There were few locations at which locomotives arrived and departed tender first. (C.R.L.Coles)

The 1848 route to Fremington is lower left and the 1854 line to Crediton is lower right. Top left is the 1874 branch to Ilfracombe. The 1905 GWR spur to connect with these former LSWR lines is on the right. The 1932 map is shown at the scale of 20" to 1 mile.

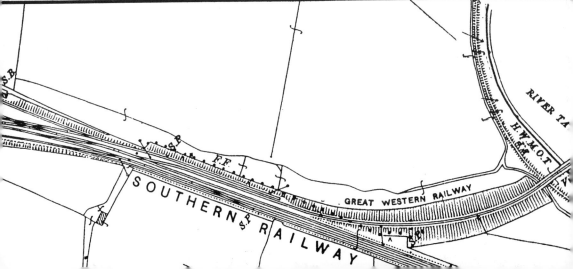

SOUTHERN RAILWAY

GREAT WESTERN RAILWAY

RIVER TA

111. No. 6372 has turned on the 50ft turntable (left) ready for another trip to Taunton on 22nd September 1955. Heaps of ash required the constant attention of the shed labourer. (T.Wright)

112. The wide Taw Valley is in the background as we watch steam activity from the island platform in 1962. Nearest to us is class 2 2-6-2T no. 41297. East Box is visible. (C.L.Caddy coll.)

113. A class M7 0-4-4T is standing by the cattle dock on 31st May 1962 as we look at the wooden engine shed, adjacent machine shop and stores. There were up to sixteen engines based here in the early 1920s. (C.L.Caddy coll.)

114. Following closure of the sheds at Victoria Road and Torrington, up to 28 locomotives were to be found here. The shed closed on 6th September 1964, one week after this photograph was taken. Note the diesel intruder. (S.C.Nash)

115. Diesels flank no. 3205 as it waits to depart with the special train on its Ilfracombe - Taunton leg. A roof for the coal stage and a mechanical loader (seen beyond it) was provided for the final years of steam. (S.C.Nash)

116. Exmoor is in the background as we examine turntable details. The horizontal handle by the cylinder of no. 7333 and the slats on the ground enabled men to push the turntable round. The lever locked it. Crews continued to sign on here until 1971. (Wessex coll.)

117. The signal box was designated "A" until 1949 when it became "East". The suffix was dropped in 1971 and the box was closed on 1st November 1987. The 40-lever frame was subsequently moved to Ropley on the Mid-Hants Railway. (J.Scrace)

118. Long disused by the railway, the wooden goods shed adjacent to the up platform was still standing and serving a useful purpose when photographed on 29th April 1992. (V.Mitchell)

119. Seen on the same day is the east end of the goods shed and DMU no. 829 enveloping itself in its own exhaust as it crawls away at 09.03. Behind it is the bridge through which trains to Ilfracombe ran until 1970 and on the left is the bridge over the route to Torrington which was used by passenger trains until 196 and china clay trains until 1982. (V.Mitchell)

**Other albums to feature Barnstaple's stations are -**
*Branch Line to Ilfracombe*
*Branch Line to Lynton*
*Branch Lines to Torrington*
*Exeter to Barnstaple*

120. Photographed in May 1992, the station still had a booking office and Red Star parcels facilities. Unusually it had cycle hire arrangements. Many railway trackbeds in the area have been adapted as cycleways for the continued enjoyment of visitors to this beautiful area. (D.Dornom)

**MP** **Middleton Press**

**Easebourne Lane, Midhurst West Sussex. GU29 9AZ**

A-0 906520  B-1 873793  C-1 901706  D-1 904474

**OOP** Out of Print at time of printing - Please check current availability **BROCHURE AVAILABLE SHOWING NEW TITLES**

Tel:01730 813169  www.middletonpress.com  email:info@middletonpress.co.uk